Time Management

Time Management Strategies And Positive Routines To
Assist You In Tracking Your Goals

*(Learn The Habit Required To Double Your Output In Half
The Time And Achieve Your Objectives Stress-free)*

Humberto Pedroso

TABLE OF CONTENT

Introduction 1

Chapter 1: Why Is Efficient Time Management So Important? 4

Chapter 2: Both Domestic And Professional 8

Chapter 3: Top Time Management Strategies 13

Chapter 4: Eisenhower's Four Quadrants Matrix 18

Chapter 5: Time Management Has Many Secrets 22

Chapter 6: Time Management For Facilitating Your Personal Development 30

Chapter 8: Avoid Becoming Distracted By Social Media. 39

Chapter 9: Why Is Time Management So Poor? 42

Chapter 10: Time Management Tools 45

Chapter 11: Personal Development Methods . 51

Chapter 12: Improved Decision-Making In The Present 54

Chapter 13: Keeping Decision Fatigue At Bay 57

Chapter 14: The Monster That Consumes Concentration 65

Chapter 15: Benefits Of Time Management 78

Chapter 16: The Capture Of Time's Thief 84

Chapter 17: Common Errors In Time Management That Are Slowing You Down.... 101

Introduction

A search for "using time effectively" returns nearly 7 million results on Google and over 9 million hits on the AltaVista web indexes. A search for "using time productively" in Amazon's book database returns over 65,000 results. There are numerous time utilisation studios and seminars.

Clearly, time and the management of time is a crucial issue, and the availability of time management products — books, articles, CDs, workshops, etc. — reflects the enormous demand for these items. The proliferation of time management aids demonstrates how commonplace time pressures have become and how desperately people are attempting to meet and find time for their obligations.

Why do so many individuals struggle so much with time management? To some extent, we are to blame for adopting a cutting-edge lifestyle. We acknowledge that a full life is a busy life, with work, family, side interests, and city obligations - all of which place genuine and conflicting time demands on us.

Many of us accept that the solution to this problem lies in cramming more exercises into each day; having more activities than time to complete them is a problem that can be addressed by becoming more efficient. If you normally complete only five of the ten items on your daily to-do list, then figuring out how to complete six will increase your productivity by 20 percent. That is fantastic if you are okay with not finishing four tasks. However, this is not time management.

Some individuals accept that the solution is to spend more time performing these ten tasks. If they are work-related, then it is necessary to spend more time at the office. Nevertheless, since time cannot be created but only redistributed, investing more energy in one action implies a reduction in another. Therefore, investing more time at work is ideal if you lack a family, social connections, leisure activities, personal interests, or the need for rest. However, this is also not time management. Essentially, it is not effective time management.

Chapter 1: Why Is Efficient Time Management So Important?

Time management is crucial because it enables you to exert more control over your working day, which in turn enables you to grow your business without compromising your ability to maintain a healthy work-life balance. Here are seven benefits of good time management:

Enhance Your Current Capabilities: After you have learned to schedule time in your day for all of your essential responsibilities, you will have a better understanding of what you must accomplish and how long each task should take. When you master this skill, you will be able to block time out of your day.

When you have a schedule to follow, you will likely find that you spend less time choosing what to focus on or procrastinating and more time performing the most important task at hand. Time management can aid in focusing on the most essential tasks and avoiding time-consuming diversions.

Make Your Work More Impressive: When you are not under constant pressure to complete a task by a certain time, you can devote more time, effort, and thought to it. Effective time management enables you to prioritise your responsibilities and guarantees that you will have enough time to complete all of your projects. When you are not rushing to complete a task in order to meet a rapidly approaching deadline, the quality of your work will improve.

Adhere to the Work Schedule: In order to effectively manage your time, you must allot specific amounts of time for each activity listed on your to-do list. Numerous individuals use time management to give themselves several extra days to complete a task or to complete it in advance of the deadline in order to have some wiggle room in the event of complications. You will always be able to meet your deadlines if you meticulously plan the amount of time required to complete each task.

Reduce Your Stress Levels: When you have a lengthy to-do list, whether for business or pleasure, it's easy to feel stressed and anxious about getting everything done. If you practise effective time management, you will be able to prioritise your to-do list and allocate sufficient time to your most crucial responsibilities. As a result, you will be aware of both the tasks that need to be completed and the amount of time you have to complete them. By prioritising your responsibilities and allowing yourself sufficient time to complete them, you will experience less stress.

Enhanced Opportunities for Professional Advancement: You may become a more reliable employee if you master time management and consistently submit high-quality work on time. In turn, this will increase your value as an employee and boost your professional reputation, which will help you discover new opportunities to advance your career.

Increase Your Self-Confidence: When you successfully meet your self-imposed deadlines and manage your time effectively and appropriately, you will gain a sense of accomplishment and confidence in your abilities. People may be motivated to improve their time management skills and pursue additional employment opportunities if they can consistently demonstrate that they have completed all of their daily tasks.

When you understand how to effectively manage your time, you will become more focused at work, allowing you to accomplish more with the same amount of time. For instance, rather than attempting to work on a significant project in the fifteen minutes before a meeting, you can instead complete a few small tasks and save the larger, more mentally taxing tasks for when you have a significant amount of time to yourself.

You will be able to work more efficiently, allowing you to accomplish more in less time.

Chapter 2: Both Domestic And Professional

Owning a business is incredibly difficult. Your attention is required by so many distractions, whereas those who work for others are never required to do so. Initially, your home-based business usually consumes a great deal of your time. Consequently, you may find it difficult to balance your obligations to your family and home life with the success of your business. It is possible to effectively balance work and family life; all that is required is balance.

Your children are an integral part of your family life. Infrequently do people who start their own businesses achieve their goal of having more time to spend with their families. Working for oneself is analogous to working for another in that both require work. You must still complete your task. Clearly, you

will likely be quite flexible, allowing you to work according to your own schedule as long as the work is completed.

You must set aside time to spend with your children. They will perceive that your new business is more important than theirs. Set aside time to engage in enjoyable activities with your children, such as visiting a park or museum during the week when fewer people will be present. If you have business-related errands that your children can assist you with, take them out to do something they enjoy, such as get ice cream or see a matinee, once you have completed your duties. This is an excellent way to recognise your children's good behaviour while you are at work.

If you have older children who can help, you can pay them to perform these menial tasks, such as filing papers and sharpening pencils. By doing so, people will feel included in your organisation and perceive that you value their presence. In order to prepare them for a prosperous future, you can also compensate them for these tasks and instruct them on business practises.

Your significant other is the additional balancing act you must perform at home. Your life will be considerably easier if your spouse is enthusiastic about your home-based business and supports all of your efforts. If the person you love is uninterested in what you are attempting to do, or even worse, resentful, the road ahead will be difficult and paved with obstacles.

Before starting a business, you should sit down with your significant other and discuss your plans. Get their feedback on the concept and let them know how much time you intend to invest in establishing your own business. You and your spouse can devise a plan to combine childcare, housework, and personal time.

No matter what, it is essential to adhere to the plan. If you've agreed to finish work at six o'clock every evening, do not immediately return to your computer after dinner to respond to emails. Occasionally, extenuating circumstances will arise; in these instances, it is essential to communicate openly and clearly to keep everyone on the same page.

When you run your own business, friends are typically your lowest priority. True friends will be patient and understanding with you. Just remember to occasionally call or write them a note to let them know that despite your busy schedule, you still care about them. When starting a home-based business, friends are an invaluable source of support; be kind to them, and you will be rewarded.

If you are dedicated and creative, a home-based business can truly provide you with everything you desire. Balance is the only requirement. Remember that you need a life outside of work, as well as the need to honour and care for the loved ones who daily support and adore you.

Chapter 3: Top Time Management Strategies

Determine a course of action by identifying your most time-consuming tasks and analysing whether or not you are focusing on the most important tasks. Realistically preparing for and estimating the time allotted for other tasks may be made easier if you are aware of how much effort is expended on typical tasks.

Creating a "to-do" list is a straightforward way to prioritise your tasks. Your lifestyle will determine if you require a daily, monthly, or annual list. Ensure that your chart does not become unmanageable. Instead of making a list of objectives or multi-step strategies, create a list of manageable sections. You can classify objects as being of high, medium, or low priority, number items in order of importance, or use a color-coding system.

Experts in time management recommend using a personal planning tool to boost your productivity. Personal forecasting techniques include planners, diaries, mobile applications, charts, notecards, portable diaries, and journals. By writing down your activities, plans, and items to memorise, you can free up your mind to concentrate on your goals. Listeners may choose to express their thoughts in lieu of speaking. The key is to select a single organised, practical solution and stick to it.

Inefficiency in time management is the result of disorganisation. Studies have shown that clutter has a negative effect on an individual's sense of well-being. Organize yourself to improve your time management.

5.1 The Eisenhower Box

Being busy does not imply that one is productive. You may spend many hours extinguishing fires, but remain uncommitted to achieving your long-term goals. This activity is time-consuming and emotionally draining. The issue is a failure to establish priorities. Regardless of the long-term benefits, humans prioritise time-sensitive tasks above all others.

The Eisenhower Structure is a fundamental decision-making tool that will assist you in distinguishing between tasks that are essential, not essential, urgent, and non-urgent. It separates tasks into four categories, indicating which should be prioritised first and which will be delegated or eliminated.

Stephen Covey popularised it in his book The Seven Habits of Highly Successful People, also known as the Urgent-Important Matrix. It was named after

America's 34th president, Dwight Eisenhower, who was known for his efficiency and organisation. Eisenhower Dwight is rumoured to have prioritised his responsibilities, as only the most vital and urgent matters reached his desk.

The Eisenhower Matrix employs this same concept to distinguish between the important and urgent tasks on your to-do list, which you can then delegate or ignore.

The basis of the matrix is the distinction between urgent and important tasks.

Urgent jobs require your urgent attention and are time-sensitive. It is a list of tasks that you feel obligated to perform. When you focus on important tasks, you become sensitive, which can make you feel protective, rushed, and constrained.

Important tasks result in the long-term missions, beliefs, and objectives of your organisation. It is possible that they will not yield immediate results. Important matters are occasionally, but not always, time-sensitive. By putting you in a receptive state of mind, focusing on essential tasks can help you feel calm, reasonable, and receptive to new ideas.

People have a tendency to believe that all urgent tasks are equally important, but this is not always the case. This misconception may be the result of our propensity to focus on immediate problems and obstacles.

Chapter 4: Eisenhower's Four Quadrants Matrix

The first quadrant is the "do" quadrant, which is where you will place all essential and significant tasks. Place in this box any task on your to-do list that must be completed immediately, has obvious consequences, and impacts your long-term objectives.

There must be no ambiguity regarding which jobs belong to this industry, as these are the ones on your mind and presumably causing you the most anxiety.

The second quadrant is the "schedule" square, where you will list all non-urgent but essential tasks. Some tasks can be deferred because they have an impact on your long-term objectives but do not need to be completed immediately.

These tasks will be completed after the tasks in quadrant one have been completed. To complete the assignment in this subject area, you can utilise a variety of time management techniques.

Quadrant 3 is the "delegate" quadrant. Here, you will place any urgent but unimportant tasks. These tasks must be completed immediately, but they have little bearing on your long-term objectives.

You may delegate these tasks to other team members because you lack a close relationship with them and they are unlikely to accept your specialised skill set. Delegating tasks is one of the most efficient ways to reduce your workload while allowing your team to acquire new skills.

After reviewing your to-do list and assigning tasks to the first three regions, you will have a few remaining tasks. The positions that have been eliminated were not necessary.

These trivial, non-urgent diversions only hinder your ability to accomplish your goals. Place the remaining items on your to-do lists in the quadrant labelled "delete."

Let's pretend Julie is the chief programme manager for a corporation of average size. She manages a large team, interacts with customers, submits reports to her superiors, is married, and has two children, all while attempting to eat and live healthily. It is reasonable to assume that Julie will not be able to achieve all of her objectives. However, she can use the matrix to determine her goals and how to deal with changes to her plans.

Chapter 5: Time Management Has Many Secrets

The rapid planning strategy is a framework for goal-oriented planning that has a significant impact on your thinking to

concentrate more on the outcome. The Rapid Planning Method (RPM) is a Result-focused, Objective-driven, and Massive-action plan. These three segments aid in obtaining better responses so that we can concentrate our efforts more effectively.

This method of time management will make it obvious which activities are time-wasting. Utilizing time-tracking apps and productivity apps, you can begin by monitoring your tasks at work. Once you have recorded your daily activities for a week, you will be able to identify all time-wasting activities and make a concerted effort to eliminate them.

While discussing time management strategies, automating repetitive tasks is one of the most effective time management techniques. If a task must be performed repeatedly, you can create repeating tasks. This will save time that would otherwise be spent manually creating such tasks.

"Do not be fooled by the appearance of your to-do list; spend your time wisely on what truly matters.

It is said that high-achievers are exceptionally coordinated. When there are a multitude of tasks to focus on, which can dilute efficiency, it can be extremely overwhelming. However, a good project management framework with an integrated task management journal can help you break down larger tasks into smaller, more manageable subtasks...

This method of time management will organise your tasks into manageable categories. With the chunks of work, you can handle your work in a manageable manner, with simple categories to deal with, and prioritise the completion of important objectives. It also facilitates the division of labour.

Would you like your time to be productive? If so, identify the most important tasks (MITs) on your daily schedule and complete them first thing.

the morning hours It is common knowledge that you have the most energy and enthusiasm in the morning. So why don't I use it to manage the largest and most difficult assignments? Similarly, once you've completed your primary responsibilities, the remainder of the day will be much easier.

Various tasks require team members to devote varying amounts of time and effort. However, because the majority of tasks received by teams today are similar, the most efficient way to manage them is to group them together.

What's the reason? Well, grouping similar or related tasks within a project allows teams to save time reorienting and complete projects faster. Custom labels can be added to strain tasks under a single label.

Most individuals procrastinate or repeatedly postpone the delivery of a project or product because they strive for perfection. It's admirable that you want to be the best at whatever task you're performing, but here's a crucial question. Do you

Have only one item on your to-do list? Obviously, the answer is "no." Since there are numerous tasks on your to-do list that must be completed simultaneously, you should stop striving for perfection and instead concentrate on completing each task as efficiently and effectively as possible.

It's fine if you don't want to upset anyone, but you should only agree to deadlines that you can definitely meet. If your schedule for the day is already full and you receive a request to complete an additional task on the same day, you should decline the request. Try not to agree to work on a project or assist a colleague until you have extra time. Keep your priorities clear and fundamental.

Everyone in the business world is familiar with the "80/20 rule" at this point. It essentially tells us that 80% of our outcomes are the result of 20% of our activities. Now, in terms of effective time management, this standard recommends that you examine your daily schedule and look for ways to simplify it. In accordance with this standard, you should

To focus on the most important tasks and complete them first.

You want to make the most efficient use of your time throughout the day, which is why you move quickly from one task to the next without pausing in between. Now, this may initially appear to be a worthwhile use of your time, but it ultimately proves to be the exact opposite. In order to maintain high levels of motivation and concentration, the human brain requires a 90-minute break every 90 minutes. Therefore, schedule buffer time (10 to 15 minutes) to complete one task and begin the next. Before returning to work, you can take a walk or read something enjoyable online to re-energize your mind.

Chapter 6: Time Management For Facilitating Your Personal Development

Self-care is an essential component of personal growth and development. Self-care is just as essential as focusing on your career and social life.

Self-care can mean different things to different people, but at its core, it entails actions that aim to improve your health, preserve important aspects of yourself, and safeguard your well-being and happiness. Though many may equate it with "spoiling" oneself, I disagree. Self-indulgence requires that you go the extra mile for yourself only after you've gone the extra mile for someone else. For instance, we often feel the need to treat ourselves after a long week of work or a stressful event in our lives. Regardless of the circumstances in your life, self-care is something you should always practise. Constantly reminding yourself of your own importance is the key to success. You make yourself more deserving and worthy of good things in life by making it a habit.

You must consistently build your self-esteem and self-confidence in the world in which we live today. And how you feel about yourself has a substantial impact and influence on how you deal with numerous aspects of your life. Therefore, when you consistently practise self-care, you consistently invest time in your personal development and self-improvement.

Chapter 7: Utilize the Eisenhower Matrix to Order Your Projects and Tasks

During his presidency, President Dwight D. Eisenhower developed the Eisenhower Matrix, also known as the Time Management Matrix, which was popularised by Stephen R. Covey in his best-selling book 7 Habits of Highly Effective People. The Eisenhower Matrix is a tool for increasing productivity that can assist entrepreneurs. It could help you prioritise the daily tasks you must complete. It is important to remember that not all of the responsibilities and activities you will undertake as an entrepreneur are created equal. Some of the tasks you complete will produce substantial results, while others will produce almost nothing. Unfortunately, both types of activities require time to complete.

The Eisenhower Matrix can help you determine which tasks should take precedence by categorising them into two groups: important and urgent. To divide tasks into two groups, you will need to understand the distinction between an essential and an urgent task. With this information, you can utilise the Eisenhower Matrix to prioritise your tasks and activities.

The Eisenhower Matrix's Four Quadrants

The Quadrant of Necessities is the first quadrant of the matrix, and it should contain tasks and activities that are both crucial and time-sensitive. These responsibilities and tasks must be completed immediately. Family emergencies and project deadlines are two examples. These are the kinds of tasks whose delayed completion can have catastrophic consequences.

Even though you cannot avoid spending time in the first quadrant, you can significantly reduce the amount of time you spend there by engaging in more second-quadrant jobs and activities.

The second quadrant is known as the Quadrant of Quality.

This sector encompasses proactive tasks that will improve or preserve your quality of life. The more time you can devote to this quadrant, the less time you will have for the other three. In this quadrant of the matrix, planning for the upcoming days and monitoring your performance to determine if you are achieving your goals are two examples of activities that would be included. The majority of these tasks are related to personal development and things you know you should be doing but are not in a hurry to complete.

The third quadrant of the matrix contains urgent but non-essential tasks and activities that will not help you achieve your goals. Reduce or eliminate as many of these tasks as you can to boost your productivity. These activities are typically draining and time-consuming. This quadrant is known as the Quadrant of Deception, and if you devote your time and energy to chores in this quadrant, you will be left wondering where your time went.

This quadrant may include tasks such as answering non-essential phone calls, responding to non-work messages, and conversing on the Internet with someone about unimportant topics. You will spend less time on the activities and tasks in this quadrant if you can learn to say "no" and delegate work to others.

Fourth and final quadrant tasks and activities are neither urgent nor significant. These tasks do not require immediate completion, and you should strive to limit or eliminate them because they contribute little to your daily progress.

This quadrant has been designated as the Waste Sector. As an entrepreneur, you must be aware of your position in this quadrant. You have reached the tipping point when you spend too much time on meaningless activities that should be reserved for your free time.

This quadrant of the matrix may include jobs and activities such as watching television, gossiping, browsing the Internet, and spending an excessive amount of time on social media.

Increasing Productivity using the Eisenhower Matrix

Important tasks add to your goals, mission, and values, whereas urgent tasks require your immediate attention. As an entrepreneur, you should concentrate your efforts on tasks that fall into the second quadrant of the matrix, i.e., those that are significant but not urgent. While the Eisenhower Matrix appears to be basic and straightforward, most people have a tendency to prioritize urgent tasks above those that aren't critical to achieving their objectives. This occurs frequently because these activities demand so much of your time and attention that you overlook the tasks and activities in the second quadrant. Place each item on your to-do list for the next day in one of the four quadrants of the Eisenhower Matrix when you sit down to make your to-do list. The tasks in the second quadrant are those that will help you progress toward your goals and for which you will need to set aside time.

Chapter 8: Avoid Becoming Distracted By Social Media.

Due to the abundance of social media platforms available today, social diversions have become more widespread. With so many options available, it is all too easy to waste hours watching television instead of concentrating on the tasks we set out to complete.

Include a time frame in your routine to help you stay focused on your objectives and avoid being distracted by social media until you've completed your obligations. If you're not distracted by social media and other unscheduled activities, you can better manage your time throughout the day. Use social media as a reward for maintaining focus and accomplishing your daily goals in order to stay on track.

Maintain Focus

The last thing you want is to spend time and effort developing a routine, only to abandon it because you've lost concentration. Putting your routine into practise requires a great deal of concentration. When you wake up in the morning with a strategy in mind, you must establish a focused mindset so that nothing can distract you. Too many individuals establish routines but fail to adhere to them; as a result, they have their plans in place at the end of the day but allow any activity to divert their attention. If you want to improve your time management skills and increase your productivity as an entrepreneur, you must be focused and determined to stick to the plan you've established for the day.

Restructure Around Time

When you reorganise your day around time, you'll find yourself making plans around the unanticipated events that can arise during your daily routine. Most people struggle with time management because they fail to account for diversions and unforeseen events, which can lead to feelings of being overwhelmed and procrastination. You will find that if you reorganise your activities according to time, you will be able to complete all of the day's activities. Developing a good routine can help you better manage your time. A schedule prevents you from wasting time deciding what to do next and clarifies what to expect throughout the day and when to expect it. After beginning a routine, you might anticipate the following benefits:

Chapter 9: Why Is Time Management So Poor?

Poor Time Management - - Have you ever questioned the time management skills of web entrepreneurs? Do we automatically accept the existence of God?

In either case, he must avoid wasting time and make the most of the flexible time that entrepreneurs have from home. If so, he may be flawed or destined for business failure.

Often, procrastination is the primary cause of poor time management, but it is not taken as seriously as it should be because it is viewed as the "creativity" of waiting. In other words, web entrepreneurs frequently fear moving business projects too quickly or making hasty decisions.

This may sound noble, but it has the opposite effect, frequently causing domestic workers to complete tasks too slowly, too quickly, or not at all. Good time management helps.

Bad time management

Planlessness in a home business is equivalent to planlessness in any other type of business. To achieve the company's objectives, a business model, a marketing strategy, and an action plan must be developed. It all depends on your ability to design and manage your time and resources efficiently, as well as your business acumen.

Daily planning may appear laborious, but when it becomes a habit, it becomes second nature. According to one study, it takes an average of 21 repetitions for a behaviour to become a habit. Once a behaviour becomes a habit, it is much simpler to maintain than to initiate something new or from scratch.

Home-based business owners operate with complete flexibility and convenience. There is no one above them who can dictate what, when, how, etc. they must do throughout the day. With so much freedom, an undisciplined individual will not know how to effectively manage time or when to say no to a specific project or new business.

Many business owners put off work and responsibilities for a variety of reasons. This can put enormous pressure on entrepreneurs to deal with or operate in a crisis mode.

Working in this manner can introduce additional, difficult-to-solve or manage issues. There are errors, incomplete projects, unmet objectives, substandard work, and even substandard business outcomes.

Chapter 10: Time Management Tools

Successful people have excellent time management skills. You can accomplish anything if you commit to using a time planner and a master to-do list. Utilizing the aforementioned time management tools and techniques on a regular basis is the best way to maximise productivity and enhance your own sense of order.

The time spent learning and mastering each one will pay off for the rest of your life through increased productivity and effectiveness.

How to Increase Your Productivity Quickly! A complimentary webinar with Brian Tracy

Utilize a planner and a comprehensive collection of lists.

Investing in a comprehensive time planner is a crucial first step in effective time management. The most effective calendars, whether printed or digital, allow you to plan your entire year, each month, each week, and even each day.

Each new project, objective, or duty should be added to your time planner's master list. Your strategy for time management will revolve around this exhaustive list. Using this master list, tasks are broken down into monthly, weekly, and daily chunks and assigned.

Employ a Checklist

Every successful executive begins each day with a master to-do list. In addition to being the most effective method for maximising productivity to date, it is also essential for achieving SMART objectives. Creating a daily to-do list begins with writing down everything that must be accomplished that day.

The general rule is that the first day of using a list will result in a 25% increase in productivity.

The simple act of writing down your tasks before you arrive at work will give you two additional hours of productive time in an eight-hour workday. The most effective method for bringing order to a chaotic situation is to create a list.

Create a comprehensive list of all the tasks you must complete today, and then prioritise them. Utilizing a time-management matrix is one method for prioritising work. Once you've organised your master list, it can serve as a road map to help you transition from morning to night as efficiently as possible. Learn the emphasis that should be placed on each task using this manual. You will develop the habit of using the list daily. Read this article on eating the frog for additional guidance.

Remember that according to the 80/20 Rule (also known as the Pareto Principle), 80% of your results will result from 20% of your efforts. In order to achieve maximum productivity, it is necessary to prioritise the activities that generate the highest returns.

Methods, Applications, and Devices for Time Management

It's fantastic that there are now so many different PDAs and electronic calendar programmes available. Regardless of the type of work performed or the industry, digital time management systems can be accessed online or downloaded to a personal computer.

Time management is the fifth step.

Learning how to effectively manage your time is a priceless skill.

There is a simple method for organising your days and weeks up to two years in advance. This organisational technique is known as the 45-file system. Using this tickler file, you can organise and plan the next twenty-four months of your life.

Here is how it works:

You will receive a box containing 45 files and 14 hanging file folders as the initial step. The following is a listing of the 45 files: The thirty-one folders correspond to the month's thirty-one days. Here you will find 12 folders, one for each month of the year (January through December). Refer to the final two files for the next two years.

This wonderful system can also be utilised with hanging files in a desk drawer.

Obtain a planner, whether digital or paper-based, and make the effort to master it. There will be substantial efficiency and convenience improvements.

Join me for a 45-minute training session titled "Kickstart Your Productivity" and I'll teach you several science-based rules I use to become a productivity powerhouse.

Chapter 11: Personal Development Methods

1. Support energy

Retaining positive words may aid in the development of more stable, positive brain networks. Why? This is due to the fact that whenever we implement positive data in our minds, our brain networks become more stable (the equivalent is valid for negative data). Therefore, retaining positive words may aid in reinforcing the neural connections between particular ideas, memories, and thoughts. This could be a straightforward way to initiate the development of energy and idealism. To attempt it, view our digital book of positive words here.

2. Outmaneuver your cell phone

Our mobile phones provide a variety of amusing content, including messages from our friends, news, games, and applications. Nonetheless, they may also be detrimental to our prosperity. This is why learning to have a better relationship with your phone and other forms of technology can be a good idea for personal development. For scientifically-based advice, consult my book Outfox Your Cell Phone.

3. Fabricate reappraisal abilities
Reappraisal is a feeling regulation technique that can assist us in rethinking what is occurring so as to decrease negative emotions and increase positive emotions. To do so, attempt to view an ongoing difficult situation in a way that is less terrible (e.g., "basically I have a roof over my head") or more positive (e.g., "this is a chance to learn and fabricate character"). The more you practise this skill, the easier it will become.

Consider more things worthy of gratitude
Practicing appreciation — or gratefulness — is a fantastic method for self-improvement. Appreciation is linked to greater prosperity and stronger

relationships. To get everything rolling with gratitude, you may need to get a gratitude journal or investigate this list of things for which to be grateful.

5. Begin a diary

Daily journaling can be an effective method for coping with challenging situations, achieving goals, and investigating thoughts and emotions in a more creative and secure manner. This article contains many additional journaling thoughts.

6. Identify and use your assets

When we set out to improve ourselves, we frequently focus on our flaws — the areas in which we may not perform as well as we would like. However, expanding our assets can also be a smart move; it can assist us in becoming extraordinary in specific capacities. Uncertain of your possessions? Here, you can locate your assets.

Chapter 12: Improved Decision-Making In The Present

For example, a young woman may decide that she wants to be successful in business as an adult. With this clear long-term goal in mind, the individual exerts significant extra effort to earn exceptional grades in high school so she will be eligible for admission to a prestigious institution. To graduate as close to the top of her class as possible, the student studies longer and enrols in more challenging courses than her peers.

After years of hard work and study, postponing the enjoyment of parties, sports, and other activities. In her personal and social life, she graduates with honours from a prestigious university and is then hired by a large company, where she has the opportunity to earn more money and advance more quickly than her classmates, who were not at all concerned about the future.

When you know exactly where you want to be in the future, it is much easier to make better decisions in the present. Generally speaking, a long-term perspective improves present-day decision-making. It is a cliche that if you don't know where you're going, any road will lead you there.

Having a long-term perspective is a highly effective trait. By looking forward into the future and back into the present, it is often possible to identify potential actions and errors to avoid. After completing this exercise, your values will be more distinct. You will be provided with the internal resources necessary to organise your schedule and daily activities so that everything you do today contributes to the formation of your ideal future.

You do not want to arrive faster if you are not moving in the desired direction. It is ineffective to manage your time in a manner that increases your rate of accomplishment if you are not moving in a direction that you have determined for yourself. Without a clear vision of the future, time management techniques and methods will only lead you to a destination that has no appeal. If you are clear on your values, vision, and mission for your life and career, as well as what you want to accomplish and the best way to do it, you can begin using some of the effective time management tools available to you.

Chapter 13: Keeping Decision Fatigue At Bay

Over time, even seemingly insignificant decisions can wear us down. Every day, we must choose how to spend every moment of our lives, including what we eat and wear, what we concentrate on, and how we spend our free time. The average person makes 35,000 decisions before retiring for the night. Every choice requires time and commitment, and we have exhausted our willpower.

Near the conclusion of a difficult project that has taken many days or even years to complete, decision fatigue is common. Until the completion of the project, you can make a large number of decisions that you have been delaying. Due to the length and intensity of the programme, people begin to act rashly and make poor decisions at this point.

5.1 Breaks that are effective versus those that are ineffective

If you want to learn and grow, you should acquire this skill, which can be taught through a variety of techniques, and take proactive steps to achieve your goals. One of these important things is taking frequent breaks from your current activities in order to improve your cognitive function. It would be beneficial if you established a routine that includes breaks from the task and time to refuel. Learn how to organise your work efficiently by heeding all of the advice.

Periods

Set a time limit, such as 30 minutes, and adhere to it. When the allotted time has expired, stop working on the project. Before returning to it or moving on to something else, pause briefly. Using this method, no matter how far along the project is, you must adhere to the deadline and stop. Because only you can determine when appropriate breaks are, you must plan ahead.

Time to Commence and Conclude

Establish and adhere to specific beginning and ending times for your tasks. When you are aware of the amount of work involved in a workday, you can allocate your time more effectively and give it value. Regardless of the amount of time allocated for the end of each day, you should always finish early.

Self-care is essential.

Frequently consume midday meals. Set a time limit and ensure that you do something completely unrelated to your current task. Never choose to work through lunch; your body and mind require rest!

Brief interludes

You should take additional short breaks, perhaps ten minutes in length, throughout the day. This is crucial if you are working on a laptop or performing any other task that requires intense concentration. Your increased energy will enhance your ability to concentrate. Moreover, it will guarantee your survival and success!

No Sudden Breaks

Take planned breaks as opposed to impromptu ones. It is crucial that you are able to prevent interruptions and develop rules in this regard. Establish and adhere to regular email check-in times, for example. Additionally, inform your family, friends, and coworkers that you are concentrating on a task and cannot be disturbed. Instead, say that you may schedule time without their presence throughout the day. You should always plan your trips!

Taking care of yourself may improve your focus and help you stay on task. Additionally, it will help you maintain your health, allowing you to always function well.

5.2 Mediation is a Treatment

Among the many benefits of meditation are that it refreshes us, heightens our awareness, makes us smarter and kinder, improves our ability to deal with the outside world, enhances communication, etc. It increases our productivity and ability to concentrate without being distracted. Your willpower will be strengthened by daily meditation, allowing you to complete daily tasks without being constantly sidetracked.

A few minutes of meditation may help you maintain composure and concentration. As a result, you were able to concentrate and work more efficiently. Exam preparation becomes easier as age increases. As a working professional, contribution to the workplace becomes increasingly important.

5.3 Providing Your Mind with the Proper Fuel

Mental degeneration is thankfully reversible. In reality, the brain is highly dynamic and capable of change at any time in our lives. You will be able to increase brain activity, reduce damage risk, and delay the ageing process! If you are willing to give your brain the nourishment it requires, you can modify your choices and decisions to some extent.

Eat significantly more

What types of energy are necessary to maintain mental acuity? Omega-3 fatty acids, found in foods like salmon, flaxseed, and walnuts, have numerous health benefits, including enhancing mental function and reducing emotional and mental disorders. These fatty acids may enhance neuroplasticity, your body's ability to change in response to stimuli, which may increase the production of particular memory- and memory-related proteins.

Purchase some green tea for your enjoyment.

Green tea is revered as a miracle beverage for the body and mind on a global scale. Due to its high antioxidant, vitamin, and mineral content, green tea is renowned for its ability to protect cells from free radical damage. It is also well-known that green tea can increase the body's metabolism and speed up its normal fat-burning processes. But did you know that daily consumption of green tea may enhance your memory, stimulate your nervous system, and improve your clarity of thought?

In a 2014 study, 12 healthy participants drank either a soda pop containing 27.5 grammes of black tea or a soda pop without any green tea. Individuals who consumed green tea performed better on tests and had enhanced connectivity between the frontal and parietal lobes of the brain, according to the findings.

Chapter 14: The Monster That Consumes Concentration

If I asked you, "What do you believe you need in order to be more productive and get more done each day?" you might respond in a variety of ways. But I want you to say, "Oh, woe is me, dear author! If only I could concentrate a bit more!" —or something to that effect.

Then, I would like to inquire, "What do you believe is the greatest enemy of concentration?" I don't think you need my assistance to complete this task. The answer is quite apparent: diversions.

You can be in the zone and intensely focused on a task, but if you receive a notification on your phone, you have to stop what you're doing to check it, and then it's difficult to get back into the zone. Numerous techniques and apps have been created over the years in an effort to combat distractions, as they are such a significant problem for many individuals.

Don't worry, you're not the only one who instinctively reaches for their phone when they hear a beep.

In this chapter, we will discuss some common types of distractions, including some that may not appear to be distractions (cough, multitasking, cough), and how to conquer this monster that devours our concentration.

What exactly are digital distractions? Simply put, digital distractions are any type of distraction that takes you out of the work mindset and is caused by technology. For instance, the majority of us carry a smartphone at all times, which is the greatest digital distraction.

I am in no way suggesting that smartphones are problematic. I am aware that the phrase "turn off your phone and live in the moment" is popular these days, but the truth is that we need our phones for the most part. We live in a world where communication, socialisation, and even work can be easily accomplished on our phones. Trying to live without it for a day or two may give you the "enjoy the moment" feeling, but it's impractical to give up your phone or social media completely.

No, I'm not anti-smartphone, but you have to admit that the fact that phones make things so easily accessible and give us so many things to do in the palm of our hands also gives them the potential to be a massive distraction.

Are you one of those individuals who reaches for their phone without much thought? And then locates and launches their preferred app in roughly three seconds? I am. I can open the YouTube app on my smartphone using only muscle memory. My finger taps on the YouTube icon seemingly of its own volition, even when I have no intention of watching anything.

It has become a routine. So how do you handle it? Let's examine a few helpful tips.

Shut it off. Thankfully, despite being the most common workplace distractions, digital distractions are also the easiest to turn off literally. If your phone is too distracting or if you get antsy if you can't immediately check a text or notification, then turn it off while you're working, or at least make adjustments.

Plan a specific time for checking your phone. If you decide to implement the Pomodoro Technique from the previous chapter, you may only check your phone during your five-minute breaks. 25 minutes is not a long time, especially when you're busy, and there's a good chance that the world did not end while you were not looking at your phone. And even if it does, you'll learn during your five-minute break.

Try reducing your intake gradually. This does not imply that you should strive to be technology-free. When you hear the notification tone and have a strong urge to check what it is, you should force yourself to wait a few minutes before looking.

Start by waiting 60 seconds, or one minute, before checking your phone. Do this every time your phone beeps (unless, of course, it's a call). After a few repetitions, increase the wait time to two minutes, then three, then four, etc.

There is no specific amount of time you must wait before checking your phone. The purpose of this exercise is to get you to a point where you are comfortable not immediately checking your phone.

I am aware that it sounds peculiar. Also, it sounds a bit dramatic, as if we are technology addicts or something.

Well... in a sense, many of us are.

Even if we believe ourselves to be well-adjusted, the mere thought of having to live without our smartphone, tablet, or other electronic devices causes a great deal of unease within us.

As dramatic as it may sound, you may want to consider weaning yourself off of your instant, automatic response to receiving a text message, email, or notification.

You know how a child with a hundred toys still wants another one because this one new toy is in some way superior to the others? Or how some adolescents desire the newest smartphone despite already possessing one that performs essentially the same functions?

This is known as Shiny Object Syndrome, and it is not exclusive to children.

It is the consistent belief that something new and "shiny" is superior to what you currently have. It is the conviction that there is always something better out there, and that we must acquire it.

Shiny object syndrome is not limited to an actual shiny object, such as a smartphone. For instance, it could be a new meal replacement shake that has recently become popular on social media. Everyone has been raving about it, so it must be of high quality. In addition, it appears to be so simple to follow because, unlike traditional diets, all you have to do is replace your meals with this shake. It's incredibly simple and the shakes are delicious, so it must be superior to your current diet, right?

Imagine yourself in that circumstance. You become convinced that this new diet is some sort of miracle that will transform your life, and you cannot wait to begin. You go to the store, buy your shakes, and begin this miraculous diet that will produce results in no time.

However, as with any healthy diet, it turns out that it takes time to see actual results. There is no instantaneous satisfaction. No before and after photos, as the majority of Instagram posts demonstrated.

Then, you begin to grow weary of the shakes themselves. They are so tedious. Then you realise that, as with any diet, you are simply consuming fewer calories than you burn. What then is the point?

So then! You can see that this new diet tea is trending!

It is a supplement, not a replacement, so unlike shakes, it will not become monotonous. It increases your metabolism so that you lose weight more quickly, and there is a website that provides suggestions for what foods to eat daily in conjunction with the diet tea to achieve weight loss! It is flawless!

You get my point, right? There will always be something superior. The grass is always greener on the other side.

You may now be wondering how this relates to a business or academic setting. Typically, it's the notion that the way you're working is inefficient compared to an alternative approach. You may be using the Pomodoro Technique, and it has been working well for you, but then you come across a YouTube video claiming that 30 minute sprints are more productive than 25 minute sprints.

You don't need to change your way of doing things, and you're not doing anything incorrectly, but you assume that something will make your life easier or otherwise better.

By the way, I'm not calling you out if you do this. With social media constantly bombarding us with life hacks and everyone claiming to be an expert, it is incredibly common for people to offer new ways to increase productivity. In the era of social media, it is simply something we must deal with on a daily basis.

So why is it negative?

Trying something new, such as a new productivity method, is not a bad thing at all. In fact, you may discover something that simplifies your life. It becomes detrimental to your work only when you make it a habit. If you find something that you strongly believe will help you because it aligns perfectly with your life and the way you work, by all means give it a shot. However, if it fails, do not simply move on to the next hack, and then, if that one fails, to the next one, and so on.

This is the point at which it becomes Shiny Object Syndrome (henceforth SOS) rather than a brilliant new idea.

SOS has a negative impact on work and productivity primarily because, to put it plainly, it wastes our time.

Consider writing a 2,000-word essay (and for dramatic effect, let's say the deadline is in four hours). Shocking horror! You have your Google Doc open and have been steadily and happily typing 500 words per hour on average.

Then, you recall a technique that promises to help you write 1,000 words per hour, and you realise that you could really use it right now. You therefore set out to find it.

You Google it, locate the page with the technique, and then read the author's entire life story before you reach the technique itself.

15 minutes have passed and you have not written a single word.

You must now learn how to execute the technique. "Make the font size small," "Make the font colour white," "Just write whatever comes to mind and edit later," and whatever other common writing advice is available, are all examples of cliche writing advice. You try it, but it feels strange, so you end up backspacing a lot, and you forget what you just wrote because you can't see it.

Another fifteen minutes have passed, and you have written perhaps fifty words. And you've just effectively wasted thirty minutes because you wanted to test out this new technique.

These writing tips are not bad, but if you haven't been following them, you'll be out of your element and find it difficult to get back into the swing of things.

Don't be afraid to try new things, but make sure you're not doing so simply because they're new, trendy, or "in" at the moment. Only proceed if you sincerely believe it will benefit you in some way.

Chapter 15: Benefits Of Time Management

The decrease in stress is the most important aspect of time management. If you adhere to time management procedures, you will achieve superior results. Even you can unwind while appreciating your work. Stress causes a disruption of the work schedule, and a disrupted work schedule can never produce the best results. No one can say whether the outcome will be good or bad with certainty.

Clearly, being productive is one of the primary objectives of time the board. When you are aware of your responsibilities, you are able to better manage them. You will be able to complete more of the right tasks in less time.

Being organised enables flexibility and adaptation. Forgotten items, specifics, and rules result in additional labour. How frequently do you have to repeat a tak? Or make an additional trip because you forgot something?

How frequently do you create your own issues? Whether it's a forgotten appointment or a missed deadline, poor time management leads to increased stress in life. Avoid creating problems for yourself by planning and preparing for your child.

When you are aware of your responsibilities, you spend less time on unproductive activities. Instead of wondering what you should do next, you are already ahead of your work.

Being on top of your time and work affords you additional opportunities. Typically, the prompt riser has more orton. Well, mollusks prefer the rrerared.

Your time management rerutation will continue you . You will be known as dependable at work and in life. No one is going to question whether you will how ur, do what you said you would do, or meet the deadline.

A common argument is that time management requires additional effort. According to the sontraru, better time management makes life easier. Thng require less exertion, regardless of whether one is pursuing a trr or completing a rrojest.

Managing your time involves allocating your time where it is needed most. Utilizing time efficiently enables you to focus on the activities that have the greatest impact on your life.

The executives will initially provide stress relief and then assist you in refocusing your efforts and improving your performance on the task. A pursued individual is more useful in less time than those who struggle more to achieve their goals in life. The goal is to have a purposeful and enjoyable life, which can be achieved by maintaining a focused perspective on everything and every step.

There is much duration in life, and it also brings about turbulence. The defining characteristic of effective time management is the ability to predict and manage outcomes. Time management does not necessitate additional skills; all you need is some knowledge and a commitment to incorporating it into your day-to-day activities.

Self-sufficiency is fundamental to human life, and self-sufficient roles consistently have a better quality of life than subordinate roles. Feeling uuallu occurs when you plan your work rrorerlu and make decisions for improvement on time. The board never takes your time, but instead gives you additional time. A person's ability to act with conviction and self-confidence propels them to the next level.

Everyone desires to attain his or her life's objective and hopes for a peaceful future after achieving it. Time management allots time where it will have the greatest impact. Time allocated by executives enables every individual to devote time to the activities that matter most to them. In this case, time management has a positive perspective on performance and making reorle sonder the planning a better option.

The limit of everubodu is the ability to differentiate only in outcomes. People who score a perfect 100 are also human and not robots; the important thing is that they pursue their dreams. When you are preparing for your next meeting and all of your tasks are listed on your to-do list, your confidence begins to wane. You may use resources to expedite the task execution process. Produstvtu is a difficult obstacle to overcome, as the rrose of rrodustvtu puts humans on their heels. It is a race that must be won by all, not just one individual. It is a wonderful thing to adorn, but the sarasvati must also manage the reure.

Chapter 16: The Capture Of Time's Thief

"Procrastination is the thief of time" is an idiom indicating that procrastinating and postponing unnecessary tasks causes individuals to waste a great deal of time. This idiom is intended to encourage individuals to act immediately, as opposed to delaying. This is possibly the most famous adage regarding procrastination and its risks, so it is useful to understand it. Consequently, the accompanying article explains this idiom and describes what delaying is and how it can be avoided.

In this variety of situations, the tardy person wastes a great deal of time postponing unimportant matters:

A person who procrastinates for several days before beginning a significant project, thereby forcing them to complete it in a hurried and unpleasant manner.

A person who procrastinates for a long time before pursuing a person they're interested in seriously, only to discover that this person has entered a relationship with another person during that time.

A person who procrastinates for a long time before beginning to work on a project they are passionate about, such as writing a book or building a business, while constantly battling the guilt and shame of being unable to make progress toward their goal.

"We are currently confronted with the presentness of tomorrow. Now presents us with its savage desperation. In this unfolding problem of life and history, the point of no return has passed for such a remarkable concept. Currently, procrastination is the time criminal. Life frequently leaves us vulnerable, naked, and despondent in front of an open door. The 'tide in men's endeavours' does not remain at flood level; it recedes. We may yell desperately for time to stop in her section, but time is deaf to our cries and continues onward. The pitiful phrase "Past the point of no return" is written atop the decaying skeletons and jumbled ruins of numerous civic institutions. There is a book of life that reliably records our attentiveness or carelessness."

Causes Of Delayed Action

Individuals procrastinate because their motivation to delay is illogically more grounded than their motivation to act. This typically occurs because their discretion and inspiration are weakened by factors such as exhaustion and delayed results, as well as by a tendency to feel temporarily better, as well as by intense topics such as anxiety and fear.

Particularly, the drive to act describes how determined individuals are to act immediately. It relies primarily on the self-control and motivation of individuals, which are affected by a variety of factors. For example, a person's restraint can be affected by how exhausted they are, while their motivation can be affected by how long they must wait before being compensated for making a move. As required, issues such as depletion and delayed results can reduce a person's composure and inspiration, and thus their motivation to act, as can numerous other issues, such as misery, ADHD, and low self-adequacy.

Alternately, the urge to delay refers to how strongly individuals feel compelled to delay action for the time being. It is predicated on the desire to feel significantly better temporarily by avoiding negative feelings (e.g., tension and dread associated with a specific task) and increasing positive feelings (e.g., enjoyment from computer games), a behaviour portrayed as "yielding to feel better". This desire can involve various fundamental issues, such as hair-splitting, which are frequently intertwined with a desire to feel better in the present.

Similarly, despite the fact that procrastination frequently causes problems with time management, it is primarily caused by difficulties with emotion regulation. Furthermore, procrastination is strongly associated with the concept of akrasia, which is a perspective in which someone acts contrary to what they would normally prefer due to a lack of adequate self-control. In light of this mental framework, we will now discuss the central points of contention that can lead to procrastination:

A substantial number of these concerns are interconnected. For instance, depression can lead to a lack of energy, a lack of energy can fuel tension, and tension can increase task aversion, delaying the proper prioritisation of the current state of mind. Similarly, the influence of anxiety on procrastination can be influenced by factors such as self-reliance and concern.

Moreover, the relationship between these issues and procrastination is complex for various reasons. For example, while certain types of hair splitting and dread tend to increase procrastination, others tend to decrease it (by expanding the inspiration to act). Depending on the situation, the precise manner in which these factors influence individuals' behaviour can vary.

Finally, keep in mind that the issues that lead to procrastination can initiate dangerous cycles. For instance, this can occur when a person is agitated about an errand, so they procrastinate on it, which makes them more agitated about similar tasks, which makes them more likely to procrastinate for a similar reason in the future.
How to Overcome Procrastination.

You might be wondering, How can I stop procrastinating? Luckily, there are various things you can do to battle procrastination and begin finishing things on time. Consider these your procrastination exercises

Make a plan for the day (To-do lists): To assist with keeping you on target, consider putting a due date close to everything.
Take small strides: Separate the things on your rundown into little, sensible advances with the goal that your undertakings don't appear to be so overpowering.
Perceive the admonition signs: Focus on any considerations of procrastination and give a valiant effort to fight the temptation. If you start to contemplate procrastination, drive yourself to put up with your assignment shortly.
Take out interruption: Ask yourself what pulls your consideration away the most — whether it's Instagram, Facebook refreshes, or the nearby news — and switch off those wellsprings of interruption.

Applaud yourself: When you finish a thing on your daily agenda on time, salute yourself and award yourself by enjoying something you see as tomfoolery.

To conquer procrastination in the long haul, do the accompanying:

You can use any combination of methods you desire, but it is best to start with the one that appears to be the most applicable to your situation. You will likely benefit from writing things down, such as your objectives and strategy. This can have a variety of benefits, including helping you think more clearly and making your decisions feel more concrete. You can use a comparative methodology as a mediation tool to help another person stop dallying by performing the aforementioned actions for them, performing them alongside them, or empowering them to do so on their own.

Finally, keep in mind that imperfect activity is generally preferable to no activity, so you will benefit more from attempting to do only a portion of the above than from doing nothing at all. In addition, the longer you wait, the more likely you are to be idle, so you should begin immediately with the understanding that you will likely misunderstand a few things at first, but that you will have the option to adjust your approach over time.

If you feel overwhelmed, start with the primary strategy in this section (focusing on a small step) until you feel ready to take on additional tasks.

Determine how you are currently investing your energy.
To improve your own time management, you must first determine where your time is going. Try recording your time

for a week by keeping track of your daily activities. This analysis will aid you in:

Determine how much you can accomplish in a day.
Time distinction stinks.
Focus on exercises that yield the highest returns.
As you conduct this time review, it will become apparent how much of your time is spent on pointless musings, discussions, and exercises.
You will gain a more accurate understanding of how much time various types of tasks require (which will be extremely useful for executing on a later tip). This exercise can also help you determine the time of day when you are most productive, so that you know when to work on tasks requiring the most concentration and creativity.

Consider the efficiency with which you budget your time. At the conclusion of your review, compare the amount of time it took you to complete specific tasks to the amount of time you anticipated they would require. We frequently underestimate how quickly things can be completed. If there is a significant difference, factor it into your future schedule planning so you can allocate your time more precisely and avoid bottlenecks and missed deadlines.

2. Develop a daily plan and adhere to it. day to day plan

This step is essential for learning how to manage time at work. Do not even attempt to start the day without a well-organized plan. Before you leave for the day, compile a list of the most pressing tasks for the following day. This step allows you to get moving as soon as you arrive at the office. Writing everything down will prevent you from tossing and turning in bed at night as you contemplate your thoughts.

Your mind works on your plans while you sleep, allowing you to wake up with new information for the following day's work. If you were unable to complete the task yesterday, be sure to create your schedule first thing in the morning. You will ensure that the time you spend making a clear arrangement isn't outweighed by the time you lose bouncing between activities when you require such an arrangement.

Concentrate on it carefully.
Prioritization is essential to effective time management when planning your daily schedule. Start by abandoning obligations that you should not be performing anyway. Then, identify the three or four most important tasks and complete them first; in this manner, you will ensure that the fundamentals are completed.

Examine your daily schedule and ensure that it is coordinated based on the significance of a task rather than its urgency. Significant obligations support the achievement of your goals, whereas dire obligations necessitate immediate consideration and are associated with the achievement of another person's goals. The majority of the time, we will prioritise urgent tasks when we should be concentrating on activities that support our business objectives.

To avoid this situation, use one of the time management tips for work found in Priorities straight by Stephen Flock. He offers the accompanying time management framework, known as the Eisenhower network, as a reliable method for concentrating on activities in light of these significant and urgent considerations.

These assignments have significant due dates and a high degree of urgency; they must be completed immediately.

Important but not Urgent: These matters are significant, but do not require immediate action and should involve long-term development planning. Invest a substantial amount of your energy in this quadrant.

These tasks are pressing, but they are not significant. Limit, delegate, or eliminate them since they do not contribute to your outcome. They are generally disruptions that may result from others' lack of common sense.

Not Urgent and Not Important: These tasks are worthless and should be eliminated as quickly as possible.

Evaluate how you are currently allocating your energy by constructing your own time management framework and incorporating elements from your daily schedule and daily exercises. You can create one in Lucidchart in less than a minute; I did it myself! When you have mastered prioritisation, your time management will reach an unprecedented level. When there are insufficient hours available, you will know where to focus your efforts. Determine how to utilise it.

Organize similar activities together.

Save time and mental energy by attempting to complete all tasks of a single category before moving on to the next. Make separate blocks of time for tasks such as noting messages, making telephone decisions, documenting, etc. Try not to respond to messages and emails, as doing so is an interruption at its finest. Turn off your phone and email alerts to eliminate the urge to check at predetermined intervals.

5. eschew the desire to perform multiple tasks.

This is one of the simplest time management tips for work, but also one of the most difficult to implement. Focus on the primary task and eliminate all interruptions. It may be tempting to perform multiple tasks at once, but doing so will only cause you to make a mess of things. Changing from one task to the next costs you time and reduces your productivity.

Do not allow a mile-long daily schedule to overwhelm you. It will not become more limited if you worry about it, so take it one assignment at a time.

6. Assign time limits to assignments.

As part of your schedule-making process, you should set time limits for assignments rather than working until they are completed. Daily agendas are ideal and brilliant, but occasionally you may feel as though you verify nothing. The Pomodoro Method can assist you in establishing a regular rhythm for your work by dividing your day's tasks into

25-minute segments, with brief breaks in between and a longer break following the completion of four segments. This strategy counteracts a lack of focus with frequent breaks, reducing mental strain and maintaining inspiration.

If you prefer to establish your own rhythm, timeboxing allows you to close off different time intervals. Utilize your time log (from Step 1) to estimate how much time an activity will require. As soon as you have expended the allotted amount of effort on that task, proceed to the next significant action. As a result of establishing these boundaries, your productivity will soar and your day's schedule will shrink.

Chapter 17: Common Errors In Time Management That Are Slowing You Down

Even though it's 3 o'clock in the afternoon, you're still working on the same modest assignment you began this morning. Your to-do list is expanding, you're running behind schedule, and it's time for two hours of consecutive Zoom meetings. Yikes. The majority of us have been in this situation, and many of us are in it on a daily basis. Despite our best efforts to efficiently plan our time, stay on top of our schedule, and complete all of our tasks, we continue to struggle to maintain order.

Instead of creating endless to-do lists, devote some time to determining the source of your time management issues. Where are you losing time, and what are you doing incorrectly? Let's examine the common errors that may sabotage your workflow and cause you to miss your deadlines.

1. Failure to set priorities

If the majority of your tasks require the same level of commitment, it can be difficult to determine which ones are the most crucial. For instance, suppose you and your team have just begun working on a high-priority project and are generating excellent ideas. A coworker interrupts you and informs you that you must attend to an urgent matter that has just arisen. It won't be easy to get into this situation, but the key is to learn how to prioritise. It takes considerable time to figure out how to do so.

2. arriving at work late

If you do not begin your day early or on time, you will be unable to fulfil your daily responsibilities. The most influential leaders have one thing in common: they are all early risers. If you begin the day late, you will almost certainly feel rushed throughout the duration of the day. Everyone's definition of "early" is different, so examine your daily routine to determine when you should begin and end your day.

Inefficient planning of activities

Our level of productivity varies from day to day and individual to individual. Others are most productive as the sun sets, while others are most productive when they first wake up. The simplest way to balance your time is to determine your peak hours and devote them to your highest-priority tasks, rather than sprinkling them with less essential, repetitive tasks.

4. exhibiting procrastination

Your greatest adversary is procrastination. Nothing is more detrimental to your concentration and true potential than circling the drain and making excuses for not getting to work. Not only does it create a massive backlog, but it also makes you feel terrible for not beginning your task, especially if it is urgent.

The most effective way to avoid this situation is to devote a specific amount of time to getting started. This will stimulate your imagination and draw your focus to the project, and you will quickly become completely immersed in it. If that fails, consider breaking the task into smaller portions.

5. failing to accurately estimate the time required to complete a task

Underestimating the time and effort required to accomplish a goal is one of the most common errors made by ambitious individuals. This is typical of A-type overachievers who believe they can control everything and never turn down a challenging opportunity.

Note the amount of time required to complete each task on your to-do list. I also propose doubling that duration. For example, if a task will take 20 minutes, allot 40 minutes. People frequently underestimate the amount of time required to complete a task.

6. Multitasking

As we strive to become more skilled at our work, we frequently fall into the trap of multitasking. Theoretically, multitasking is possible if you need to stay on top of your workload.

Multitasking, on the other hand, prevents you from focusing equally on all of your responsibilities and takes significantly longer than completing tasks sequentially. To put it another way, if you want to be proficient at multitasking, you must be well-organized and possess a high level of concentration, creativity, and accuracy. Multitasking is not for everyone; therefore, choose your battles carefully. When possible, refrain from multitasking and focus on a single task. This will help you produce high-quality work and give you a feeling of accomplishment.

Being productive as opposed to being occupied

As much as we'd like to remain focused on high-priority tasks, we occasionally lose sight and end up performing a number of low-priority tasks that not only consume our energy and time, but also have little or no effect on the outcome we're aiming for. If you have several small tasks to complete, group them together. Complete three days' worth of minor tasks in a single afternoon, as opposed to one activity per day.

8. Taking too many breaks

Set aside time for breaks whether you're working on a high-priority task or a series of low-priority tasks; our brains were not designed to concentrate for eight hours straight. The only acceptable option is to take a break and engage in non-work-related activities, such as eating, taking a short walk, exercising, or simply resting. This should help you clear your mind and acquire more mental energy for the upcoming work. Planning is the key to high levels of productivity. Spending time creating a to-do list, blocking off your schedule, and prioritising tasks may seem like a waste of time when you're overworked, but planning will save you time and stress in the long run.

www.ingramcontent.com/pod-product-compliance
Lightning Source LLC
Chambersburg PA
CBHW050300120526
44590CB00016B/2427